The Granary The____
*present_*

Tilt

by Ailís Ní Ríain

AIRNIN Rachel O'Shea
OLAN Aidan O'Hare
EANNA Hannah Burke

Director Graeme Maley
Lighting Designer Julie Kearney
Sound Designer Brian Docherty
Stage Manager Laura Cockett

The New Works

GRANARY

DISCARDED

BIRMINGHAM CITY UNIVERSITY

17 – 21 April 2007
Open Eye Gallery, Liverpool

24 – 28 April
Granary Theatre, Cork

1 – 5 May
Citizens' Theatre, Glasgow

Hannah Burke (*Eanna*)

Hannah graduated from East 15 Acting School in June 2007. Theatre during training includes: *A View from the Bridge*; *Richard III*; *Lower Depths*; *A Flea in Her Ear*; *Live Like Pigs*; *Major Barbara*. Film credits include: *Death by Misadventure*. Other theatre credits include: *Skolka* (Point of Departure) and Oisin in *Tir Na Nog* (Clan Cluana). Hannah is very pleased to be making her professional debut in *Tilt*.

Aidan O'Hare (*Olan*)

Since graduating from Manchester Metropolitan's School of Theatre, Aidan has enjoyed a diverse career in theatre, television and film. Most recently he starred in Ken Loach's 2006 Palm d'Or-winning *The Wind That Shakes the Barley*, as Steady Boy. Other TV and film credits include: *Conspiracy of Silence* (independent film); *Feel the Force* and *Switch* (both BBC). Aidan's theatre credits include *The Shadow of Gunmen* (Citizens' Theatre); *Duck* (Royal Court Theatre and national tour); *Ladies and Gents* (Brighton Festival); *Blue* (Latchmere Theatre); *Crystal, Losing Steam* and *The Tempest* which were all performed at the Midsummer Festival in his hometown of Cork, Ireland. Other credits include: *Scenes from an Execution*; *Our Country's Good*; *The Devils*; *Grimm's Tales* and *Samburi* (African tour).

Rachel O'Shea (*Airnin*)

Rachel was born and raised in Cork, and trained at Bull Alley in Dublin and at the Gaiety School of Acting, and on further courses at the Irish Film Actors Studio and in Stanislavsky's system at the Focus Theatre. Theatre credits include: Doreen in *Having a Ball*; Mary in *Low Level Panic*; Ellie in *Heartbreak House*; Madelaine in *Desert of Love*; Joan in *Forty-Four Sycamore*; Sherbet in *Fastest Clock in the Universe*; and Diana in *Venus with a Filthy Hangover* and Katherina in *Amadeus* (Samuel Beckett Centre). Film credits include: Julianna in *Chess* (Inspired Movies); Rachel in *Sex and Sensibility* (Athena Films) and many more short and feature-length films including *Black Deception* (Samson Films). Television credits include: *Fair City* and Alice in eighty-two episodes of *Awaaz* (Zee Television).

Ailís Ní Ríain (Writer)

Born in Cork in the Irish Republic, the international prize-winning composer Ailís Ní Ríain combines her interests as a composer, devisor and writer to produce works which challenge, provoke and engage. She is particularly interested in cross-discipline collaboration, opera, music-theatre and presenting contemporary music in diverse spaces. Her music has been performed throughout Europe and the USA and on Irish, Greek and German radio. She has been represented by the Contemporary Music Centre of Ireland since 1999.

Her composition *StreetSong* won joint-first prize at the 2006 ISCM* World New Music Days Short Cuts: Beauty Competition in Stuttgart (*International Society of News Music). *EXIT* was placed second in the Vienna Modern Masters: 2006 Nancy Van de Vate International Composition Prize for Opera. Recent commissions included *Surrealist Pilgrims* for amplified cello and tape for the National Concert Hall of Ireland in March 2007 and *Into the Sea of Waking Dreams* for the Living Composer's Project, and *10,000 Deviants* for Eleven Ensemble.

Although her formal training has primarily been in classical music as a composer and pianist, Ailís has been writing texts for several years, often incorporating these within her musical compositions, her particular interest being in voice theatre and soundscape. More recently she has been focusing on writing for performance and in November 2006 Ailís was selected as one of the most promising UK-based emerging writers to attend the Cubed3 Writers Residency at the Traverse, Scotland's new-writing theatre.

Her poetry has been published by many publications including *Citizen 32, Lamport Court, Aesthetica Magazine, The Argotist, The Ugly Tree, Papercut, This is it* and *Parameter*. For more info visit www.ailis.info.

Graeme Maley (Director)

Director of The New Works; productions include *Red* by Chris Fittock, (Liverpool, Glasgow Citizens' Theatre and Theatre 503 London) and *The Doll Tower* (Unity Theatre Liverpool) by Ronan O'Donnell. Previous work includes: *h*, 16mm black and white mute picture, Liverpool Culture Company/Liverpool Philharmonic Hall; Assistant Director Traverse Theatre; *Cactus Milk*, Klink and Bang/Garpur Iceland; *Picasso's Women*, Assembly Rooms Edinburgh Festival; *Macbeth*, Lemon Tree Aberdeen; *The Danny Crowe Show*, Dundee Rep; *Brazil*, Latchmere Theatre London and Arches Glasgow; *Great Moments of Discovery*, Paines Plough; and *The Ballad of James II* (reading) The Scottish Playwrights, Studio Stirling Castle.

Julie Kearney (Lighting Designer)

Julie graduated from the Liverpool Institute for Performing Arts in 2003. During her time at LIPA Julie lit a variety of shows including *Godspell*, *Songs For A New World*, *Guys and Dolls*, *All My Sons*, *Company* and *Beautiful Thing*. *Beautiful Thing* was entered into the 2004 National Student Drama Festival, and won the Stage Electrics Best Lighting Design award. Julie also designed an installation, *Twirly Stairs*, which was in situ in a glass fronted spiral staircase within LIPA, photographs of which have been published and used in various promotional materials for LIPA. Other shows lit by Julie include Urban Memoirs (commissioned by the Arts Council), *Ms Ross*, *The Lady and Her Music*, *Tina Duckett Says...*, *Bugsy Malone*, *AOG Conference*, *Breakout*, *Procter Dance Showcase*, and *Spooky Days*.

Brian Docherty (Sound Designer)

Previous theatre works include *The Doll Tower*, *Brazil*, *If Destroyed True*, a couple of Shakespeares, National Theatre of Scotland *Home* (Glasgow). *Something in Iceland*. Sound Installations in GOMA and Kelvingrove Art Gallery. A musical called *Giacomo's Circus of the Fantastic* for RSAMD. Producing and writing albums this year with

MC Soom, T James Kirk and Serf. Currently Musician in Residence in South Lanarkshire.

Laura Cockett (Stage Manager)

For the past few years Laura has worked as a freelance stage manager working with a variety of companies both in the UK and in Europe. Recent stage management credits include *Urban Strawberry Lunch*, tours with Walk the Plank, operators of Britain's only touring theatre ship, and with Producoes Supplementares, a company of international artists based in Portugal.

Thanks

The New Works would like to thank:
Arts Council England North West;
Liverpool Culture Company;
the Peggy Ramsay Foundation
and the Garfield Weston Foundation
for continuing to support the production
of our new work.

The New Works would also like to thank
Nick Hern for choosing to publish *Tilt*.

Thanks to the Arches Theatre, Glasgow;
Patrick and Stephanie at Open Eye Gallery, Liverpool;
Tony and staff at Granary Theatre Cork;
Jeremy Raison and staff at Citizens Theatre, Glasgow;
Unity Theatre, Liverpool; Crystal Stewart;
Alan at Hope Street, Liverpool; Matt Applewhite;
Vashti McGlachlan, Eoin Geoghegan and
Ronan O'Leary for their creative work, The Club.

Liverpool 08
EUROPEAN CAPITAL OF CULTURE

The New Works

Literary Director   Chris Fittock
General Manager   Nicki Green
Director   Graeme Maley

To find out more about The New Works,
you can go to our website,
www.thenewworks.com
where you can also leave messages
and comments in The Green Room.

An important source of information about new writers
and their work comes from the unsolicited scripts that
we receive. We welcome scripts from all writers in the UK
and will consider all pieces submitted to The New Works.
Please send your scripts to: Chris Fittock, The New Works,
1 Hope Place, Liverpool L1 9BG, enclosing an SAE.

Recent Productions

Red
by Chris Fittock, 2006

'A tremendous frightening force-field
of a seventy-minute drama . . . The acting is superb
throughout Graeme Maley's flawlessly
simple production. ****'   *The Scotsman*

'Pure animalistic need pulses and throbs
throughout Fittock's chewy text . . . styled like
some undiscovered Greek tragedy'   *The Herald*

The Doll Tower
by Ronan O'Donnell, 2005

'Sterling scripting, acting and production standards . . .
a feat in its own right. 9/10'   *Liverpool Echo*

TILT

Ailís Ní Ríain

2

Characters

They are three. They are siblings. They are pale, blond and small of stature. Each has a scar on his or her face. Each plays him or herself as a young child, as a teenager, and as an older adult. They have strong Southern Irish accents.

AIRNIN. *Female, the youngest. A tomboy. Her movements range from bird-like and speedy to completely static. She has long blonde hair, which she wears loose and unkempt, and a red scar that runs as a short line under her right eye. She has the mid-range voice of the three.*

OLAN. *Male, the middle child. He is physically sturdy, broad-shouldered, but not taller than the others. He has a burn scar on one side of his face and upper body. He has very short blond hair and has the deepest voice of the three. He moves energetically, with confidence, and is often volatile.*

EANNA (*pronounced ee-an-na*). *Male, the eldest. He is the slightest of the three, with the lightest voice. He has slightly floppy hair and moves tentatively and awkwardly. He has a red scar running over the bridge of his nose and his left arm is partially paralysed; he holds it up as if it is in a sling, and this limits his physical movement considerably.*

Their scars should not look fresh; they are permanently red and have not faded. Their skin should not look bruised in any way.

The action is not set in a particular time or place.

Scene One

Pace: lively with bright energy.

They are young children.

AIRNIN (*a sudden memory*). Mirage!

EANNA. What is that you're sayin'?

OLAN. Some class of a vision?

EANNA. Or an illusion?

AIRNIN. No, lads – the dog! D'ya not 'member?

EANNA (*gathering pace*). I 'member he was no hallucination!

OLAN. No delusion.

EANNA. No optical illusion.

OLAN. No figment of our imagination.

AIRNIN. Jesus, he was a beautiful dog . . .

EANNA. But he sure had a manky name!

OLAN. Sure, who in God's name would give a dog a name like that?

AIRNIN *and* EANNA (*as if obvious*). The Jerries!!

AIRNIN. Sure wasn't he a German shepherd, trained by an ex-SS officer?

OLAN. Suppose you're right there, Airnin!

EANNA. A German shepherd who was actually German!

AIRNIN. You're not wrong there, Eanna!

OLAN. Jesus! That dog was something else though, wasn't he, lads?

AIRNIN. 'Member the way he'd react to the ol' German commands . . .

EANNA. Ya couldn't make it up, ya couldn't make it up!

AIRNIN. You surely could not, sure who'da believe ya?

OLAN. 'Member the Jerry threatened to shoot him if the Da Da didn't take him off his hands?

AIRNIN. Jesus, that guy was a luner!

EANNA. Bloody looper-loo!

OLAN. Total askew!

AIRNIN. Could nothing be simple in that house?

EANNA *and* OLAN (*with humour*). NO!!

AIRNIN. Three little blondie childer speakin' German to a big bloody dog in the bowels of County Cork.

EANNA. Total askance, boi!

The following is playacting. The translations are not spoken.

OLAN. Herkommen, herkommen! [*Come here.*]

AIRNIN. Sitzen! [*Sit.*]

OLAN. Hervorholen! [*Fetch.*]

AIRNIN. Sitzen!

OLAN. Bellen! [*Bark.*]

EANNA. Woof!

AIRNIN. Herkommen, herkommen!

EANNA. Woof, woof!

OLAN. Hervorholen!

AIRNIN *and* OLAN. Herumrollen, herumrollen, herumrollen, herumrollen!! [*Roll over.*]

AIRNIN. Bloody tick-tick-tocker-boi!!

OLAN. Sure, no one would believe it!

AIRNIN. Could nothin' be simple in that house?

OLAN. Not in the war zone with the tea- and coffee-making facilities and the fully stocked bar in the living room!

EANNA. Not forgettin' the tennis court.

OLAN. Or the sauna.

AIRNIN (*stresses to* OLAN). It was a war zone.

OLAN. Or the games room!

EANNA. Or the swimmin' pool out the back!

OLAN. A fine war zone for a neutral nation!

EANNA. Nothin' by halves, wa?

OLAN. The privilege!

EANNA (*manically*). Nothin' by halves ha, ha, ha, ha!

OLAN. Oh what privilege! Hey, hey, hey, hey!

Pause.

AIRNIN (*bitterly*). We were privileged indeed . . .

Long pause. Slower.

OLAN (*slowly*). I'll never forget what happened in the swimmin' pool out the back . . .

AIRNIN (*kindly*). Sure, that's a long time ago now, Olan.

EANNA. Yeah, sure, that doesn't matter now, boi . . .

OLAN (*tetchily*). How can you say it doesn't matter?

Pause.

Pace: lively.

EANNA (*changing the subject*). Hey! The cars. Jesus! The cars!

AIRNIN. What cars?

EANNA. He loved his cars, didn't he, lads?

AIRNIN. What are you sayin' there now, Eanna?

EANNA. A new one, twice a year . . .

AIRNIN. The Da Da was always havin' to have the biggest and the best . . .

OLAN. And why not, lads, didn't he work for it?

AIRNIN. There are more important things, Olan.

EANNA. Always the latest model. (*To* OLAN.) Would you call that a fetish?

OLAN. Or more of an obsession?

EANNA. The Da Da always *had* to drive the latest model –

OLAN. Nothin' less would do . . .

EANNA. Or a compulsion?

OLAN. A queer addiction of sorts?

AIRNIN (*sardonically*). Even before the thing was built the Da Da had to have it . . .

EANNA. Jesus, he was demented!

OLAN. I'd say it was more of a mania.

AIRNIN (*melting*). Well, he did have a touch of the ol' tick-tockers!

EANNA (*pensively*). But how many cars could one man need at any one time?

AIRNIN. Ah, men like their cars, Eanna.

EANNA (*decided*). No, I'd say it was more of an addiction.

OLAN. Yeah, probably more of an addiction alright . . .

EANNA. T'after all, he didn't take a drink, did he?

OLAN. No. Sure he only had the two hobbies, the cars . . .

EANNA. . . . and beatin' us all up!

Pace: very fast.

*Mimicked, snappy, manic, rhythmic to *.*

AIRNIN. What to do?

OLAN. When you don't have a clue!

AIRNIN. And all around you there's black and blue!

OLAN. A lovely hue, a lovely hue!

AIRNIN. Black-blue is the colour of my young love's face. Hee, hee!

OLAN. Hey, hey!

AIRNIN. Never a day went by without some little 'accident'.

OLAN. Some little 'incident' of kin.

AIRNIN. Oh, you'd never be done with the troubles of the interior!

OLAN. Never be done!

AIRNIN. Be done, done, done!!

OLAN. With the beatin's!

AIRNIN. With the biddy-bid beatin's. *

Long pause.

Pace: moderate.

AIRNIN (*matter-of-factly*). So, that was the story.

EANNA (*amazed*). You couldn't make it up!

AIRNIN. You surely could not.

EANNA. 'Tis unbelievable!

AIRNIN. 'Tis unbelievable alright.

EANNA. Never heard the likes of it . . .

AIRNIN. And you won't again.

EANNA. Jesus, that's for sure!

AIRNIN. Sure, who'da believe ya?

EANNA. Sure, who'da believe ya is right!

OLAN (*tetchily*). What is that you're sayin'?

EANNA (*to* OLAN). Just sayin' that that story there takes some beatin', Olan.

AIRNIN (*smugly*). Well, that *was* the story.

EANNA (*hanging off her every word*). Was it a long story?

AIRNIN. 'Twas a long story . . .

EANNA. . . . that took some beatin'?

AIRNIN. 'Twas a very long story that took some . . .

OLAN (*sharp interruption*). Short temper.

Pause.

AIRNIN (*tense*). He had.

Pause.

(*Trying to change the subject.*) Ah, long time ago now, boys . . . Back to myself – sure, wasn't that the story after all?

EANNA. Ah, indeed'n it 'twas Airnin, indeed'n it 'twas.

AIRNIN. A long walk back to myself from it all . . .

EANNA (*losing conviction*). Back to yourself from it all . . .

OLAN. Why did he do it?

EANNA (*ignoring the question*). Such a sharp . . .

OLAN. What?

EANNA. . . . stinging . . .

AIRNIN. What?

EANNA. . . . beating . . .

OLAN. What?

Pause.

EANNA. . . . heart.

Pause.

AIRNIN. It's a long story. A long story of the Da Da's short

servitude to our Mammy and his paralysin' punishments for
nothin' at all.

Pause.

OLAN (*up for it*). Maybe she asked for it?

AIRNIN (*sharply*). Back to myself.

OLAN (*sardonically*). Sure, wasn't that was the story after all?

EANNA (*deep in thought*). After all she'd been through . . .
A warrior.

OLAN. Beaten like a dog . . .

EANNA. A warrior . . .

AIRNIN (*warning*). We don't speak about it.

OLAN (*sharply*). You don't speak about it . . .

Pause.

Pace: lively, gradually becoming hysterical.

One day there was a daisy in the lawn. One tiny daisy. One-
acre lawn.

EANNA (*quickly, half-whisper*). Was it enough?

OLAN. The very sight of it was enough!

EANNA (*becoming unhinged*). Enough to make him blow?

*Childlike, getting carried away, over the top. OLAN
playfully hits EANNA.*

OLAN. Battered!

EANNA (*hits OLAN, timidly at first*). Blasted!

OLAN. Bashed!

EANNA (*getting into it*). Bruised!

OLAN. Bloody!

EANNA. Broken bones!! (*He rubs his arm.*) Ha, ha!

OLAN. Hey, hey! You've got to watch out for them daisies,
Missus, whatever you do don't let one grow!!

EANNA. If you do nothin' else –

OLAN *and* EANNA. DON'T LET ONE GROW!!

Pause.

AIRNIN (*innocently*). But isn't that what daisies do?

Pause.

OLAN. Hey, d'ya 'member when the Big Man used to take to the bed, lads?

EANNA. Yeah, he'd be often fierce down in himself alright . . .

OLAN. Goin' like the clappers for six months and then without a sneep he'd about-turn and take to the bed for the next six . . .

EANNA. Sure, isn't that one of the perks of being your own boss? You can break down on your own terms and in your own time!

OLAN. That's it in the shell of a nut!!

EANNA. In the shelly of a nut-nut!!

AIRNIN (*seriously*). Wasn't the house a different place when he took to the bed though, lads?

EANNA. 'Twas a sort of queasy quietness to it alright – you could never relax.

OLAN (*playacting*). Because you never knew –

EANNA (*rising*). You never knew –

OLAN *and* EANNA. When he would BLOW!!

AIRNIN. Many's a day the Mammy spent in the A&E in her posh frock . . .

OLAN (*in a camp 'posh' mother voice*). Doctor, how dare you suggest such a thing! Do you not know who I am?

EANNA (*manic whisper*). Did he not know who she was?

OLAN. I simply walked into a door. I resent your accusations!

AIRNIN (*similar whisper*). Did he not know who she was?

OLAN (*in his normal voice*). She changed doctors. The new one didn't know who she was. He useta call her the door woman . . .

EANNA. 'Twas a pity she didn't manage to walk through a few more of them then, wasn't it?

OLAN. That would have solved a lot alright!

EANNA (*in an undertone*). 'Twould.

Short pause.

(*Suddenly scared.*) Maybe we shouldn't speak about it . . .

OLAN. Maybe we should . . . (*Pause.*) She could have left – surely with all that money she didn't have to put up with the biddy-bids?

AIRNIN. But she did leave.

EANNA. Ya, but she came back . . .

OLAN (*becoming angry*). For more? For a few more rounds in a losing battle?

EANNA. Why did the ol' mole come back, Airnin?

AIRNIN. Because of . . .

OLAN (*challenging*). 'Because of' – ?

AIRNIN. . . . us.

OLAN. She should have taken us with her.

Short pause.

EANNA (*anxious, upbeat, to* AIRNIN). Anyway! Back to you, Airnin, always back to you, girl!

OLAN. She was riskin' our lives and hers.

EANNA. 'Tis your story after all . . . No need to be speakin' about all that t'udder stuff at all.

OLAN (*to* EANNA). Don't *you* 'member what happened in the swimmin' pool out the back?

AIRNIN (*realises what's coming*). How could you forget what happened in the swimmin' pool out the back?

OLAN (*to* EANNA). D'ya 'member her floatin' in red in the swimmin' pool out the back?

EANNA (*clearly uncomfortable*). We don't speak about it.

AIRNIN (*as a small child, becoming manic*). Mammy, what are you playin' at?

OLAN (*similarly*). Are you playin' at dead, Mammy?

AIRNIN. What's with the red, Mammy?

OLAN. Mirage went mad . . .

AIRNIN. . . . tryin' to pull us from our beds . . .

OLAN. . . . after pullin' her from the pool . . .

AIRNIN. . . . barkin' tick-tock hysterical –

OLAN. Tryin' to wake us up . . .

EANNA (*pained*). I never saw her so white . . .

OLAN. 'Member the Mammy lyin' by the side of the status symbol?

AIRNIN. Whiskey-breath chlorine . . .

EANNA. Her bruised breasts blossoming green.

OLAN. The three of us in various states of play –

Each childlike and highly animated to *.

AIRNIN. Mammy! What's goin' on?

OLAN. Breathe, why don't you?

AIRNIN. Come on out of that now, Mammy!

EANNA. Breathe, Mammy!

AIRNIN. What game is this you're playin' now, Mammy? Stop your coddin'!

EANNA. You're goin' a funny colour, Mammy! You're goin' a funny colour!

AIRNIN. Stop your coddin' now, will ya?

OLAN. Breathe, why don't ya?

EANNA. Whiskey-breath chlorine . . .

AIRNIN. Breathe, Mammy!

ALL (*shouting*). BREATHE, MAMMY!! *

    Pause. Slower.

OLAN (*as himself, sardonically*). Privileged indeed . . .

    Short pause.

EANNA (*as himself, matter-of-factly*). They say she drank.

AIRNIN (*confidently*). They say the Pope's a Catholic.

OLAN. They say she had it comin'.

AIRNIN. They say the sun rises and sets.

EANNA. They say she knew what he was like before it began.

AIRNIN (*in a 'posh' professor voice*). In the beginning there was *neychar*! [*Nature.*]

OLAN (*pointedly*). They say she could have left.

    Pause.

AIRNIN (*as herself, sardonically*). They say the moon is made of cheese . . .

    Pause.

    Pace: very slow, as it they are floating in space.

EANNA (*introspectively, sotto voce*). We.

OLAN. Three.

AIRNIN. Are.

EANNA. One.

    Short pause.

ALL (*whispered*). We three are one.

    Pause.

EANNA (*quietly*). Maybe it's best not to talk about it . . .

Pace: brisk, upbeat.

AIRNIN. 'Tis best not to talk about it.

OLAN (*making his point*). He tried to kill her that night.

AIRNIN (*sing-song*). It wasn't the first time.

EANNA (*similarly*). It wasn't the last . . .

OLAN (*to* EANNA). He'd tried to kill you.

AIRNIN (*to* OLAN). You took some beatin's yourself!

OLAN. What are you talkin' about?

AIRNIN. Sure, you were as likely to get a puck as any of us, the Mammy included.

OLAN (*inflated*). Naw, girl, he could see that I was the tough one!

AIRNIN. Jesus, Olan, would you stop deluding yourself, boi!

OLAN (*ignoring her, military-like*). Obliteration! Eradication! Extermination!

EANNA. Of who?

OLAN (*to* EANNA). Of you.

EANNA. Of me?

OLAN (*with a nod to* AIRNIN). And her.

AIRNIN (*to* OLAN). And you!

EANNA. All of us . . .

OLAN. Jesus, it's a wonder we're still here at all.

Pause.

*Pace: medium. They speak in 'posh' Cork adult voices to *.*

AIRNIN. Those children had everything.

OLAN. The best of schools.

EANNA. The best of clothes.

AIRNIN. All the latest gadgetry.

EANNA. The best of the best!

OLAN. Not forgettin' the swimmin' pool.

EANNA. Or the tennis court out the back. *

As themselves, sardonically.

Pace: gathering intensity.

AIRNIN. Yes, siree! Not forgettin' the freeloaders now . . .

OLAN. Or the hangers-on.

EANNA. Or the fair-weather friends.

AIRNIN. Or the abusers of kind.

OLAN. They knew when to leave!

EANNA. Oh, they certainly did!

AIRNIN. Happy days indeed . . .

EANNA. Smacky, wacky. . .

OLAN. . . .wallopy days!

AIRNIN. Black 'n' blue . . .

EANNA. . . .'n' grey days . . .

AIRNIN. We were privileged indeed!

OLAN. Black 'n' blue . . .

EANNA. 'N' blue 'n' grey days . . .

AIRNIN. Tell me this lads and tell me no more: where did all the fair-weathers go?

OLAN. They weren't long runnin' when things got ugly!

EANNA. And they didn't come back, did they? Jesus, we were losing pally-pals by the new time . . .

OLAN. I'd smash a few of their heads together now if I had the chance, I'm telling ya.

AIRNIN. There for the good times and nothin' else. (*To* EANNA.) 'Twas no wonder you took to your room for as long as you did, Eanna, you lost out bad.

EANNA. I only had the one friend, I couldn't understand why he was stayin' away from the house at all . . .

OLAN. Sure Jesus, they were scared of the Da Da, ya cripple! They'd see his temper, take one look at your arm, put two and two together and they'd be outta there!

EANNA. D'ya think that's what is was, Olan? D'ya think that's why's we had no pals?

OLAN. I'm tellin'ya, if I saw them now I'd beat them from this fuggin' world to the next, so I would. I'd rip out their selfish eyeballs and make them eat 'em.

AIRNIN (*with a wink to* EANNA). Olan, you're such a big man, aren't ya?

OLAN (*getting carried away and very graphic*). Then I'd shove a stick right up their tight arses and start twistin'!

EANNA. Jesus, that would show them alright, Olan!

AIRNIN *is looking amused throughout the following. While* EANNA *becomes more animated than we have seen him,* OLAN *becomes vicious.*

OLAN (*as if he is the authority on the subject*). Then to the strappado, also known as the pendulum, where I'd bind their wrists behind their back, toss a rope over a beam, then drop 'em from it repeatedly till their arms and shoulders dislocated.

EANNA. Go on, go on, Ol! What would ya do next?

OLAN. Next would be the squassation, Eanna. This is where I'd hang the biggest weights I could fuggin' find from them – the greater the weight, the more bones would dislocate.

EANNA (*overexcited*). Go on, go on, Ol!!

OLAN. Then I'd impale the fuggers, rip off their buggerin' ears and stick 'em through their ma's letterboxes.

EANNA (*out of control*). You tell 'em, boi, you tell 'em!!

OLAN. Here ya are, Missus, here's what's left of your little rut, your manky childer, the soot of your soul, what should have been aborted through your fuggin' gaping hole.

EANNA. You tell the fuggers! You tell the fuggin' fuggers!!

OLAN (*furiously*). I fuggin' hate ya! I fuggin' hate ya all!

Pause.

AIRNIN (*to* OLAN *who is trying to pretend he is not upset*). You were always bein' the big man, weren't ya, Ol? But he got to ya too, though, didn't he?

EANNA (*subdued*). They all knew we were trash underneath the money . . . that's why they stayed away . . . they knew we were trash, sure, who'd want to be around any of us?

Pause.

AIRNIN (*wearily, but resigned to go on*). Well, back to myself.

OLAN (*challenging*). Is this only your story?

AIRNIN (*ignoring him*). We've a way to go yet, boys.

OLAN. Is it only your story, Airnin?

EANNA (*innocently*). Where are we going?

Scene Two

Pace: lively.

They are teenagers.

OLAN *speaks as the Father, as if at the breakfast table, holding up a slice of toast in the shape of a triangle.* AIRNIN *is nearby,* EANNA *is watching this scene from afar.*

OLAN. I'm the Da Da – otherwise known as the boss 'round these here parts! (*Pause, to* AIRNIN.) Hey, Missus. Missus!

AIRNIN (*as Mother*). What's that you're sayin' now?

OLAN (*as if stating the obvious*). Wrong shape . . .

AIRNIN. What are ya meanin' to say by that?

EANNA (*as himself*). She should have known, then it wouldn't have had to happen . . .

OLAN (*incredulous*). Missus! (*Gradually becoming hysterical.*) What's wrong with this toast, Missus?

AIRNIN. I don't know what ya mean.

OLAN. It's the wrong shape, Missus! (*Manically.*) You've only gone and cut 'em into triangles! Do ya not know that I only like soldiers, sure I hate triangles! How many times does I have to tell ya! (*He hits her across the face.*) How many times??

EANNA (*mimicking 'Father'*). Didn't she know he only liked soldiers, sure he hated triangles?

OLAN. How many times do I have to tell ya that I only like soldiers, I hate triangles!! (*He hits her again.*) Must do better, Missus, must do better! Must do something about the shape of this toast!

EANNA (*similarly*). Must do better, Missus!

OLAN *hits her again. She falls.*

OLAN (*softer*). Sure do I ever have triangles? Don't I always have soldiers??

EANNA (*as himself*). The ticky-tock madness of it. He should be locked up in a rubber room.

As OLAN *is kicking* AIRNIN, *as Mother, in the stomach:*

Her head hits that floor so fast her blood spatters my cornflakes. Then she does what she always does –

AIRNIN *follows these directions as he speaks:*

– tried hard to hide her indignity, pulls her skirt down over her knees, struggles to her feet, avoidin' eye contact with us, cleans herself up, clears up the mess, while he eats his eggs and leaves the toast . . . (*Pause.*) Why don't you say somethin', Mammy? Why are you takin' this shite from the thick bastard? Go on, say somethin', Mammy. Now's your chance!

AIRNIN (*blood streaming down her face*). What do you want for lunch?

Pause. Slow.

OLAN (*as himself*). Something must have provoked him to turn on her like that.

EANNA. He was the devil incarnate . . .

OLAN. I mean she musta done something wrong . . .

EANNA (*seeing red*). The devil himself.

Pause.

AIRNIN (*as herself*). Why does the Mammy drink so much of the rotgut?

OLAN. She sure knows how to put it away alright, doesn't she?

AIRNIN. Some days she reekin' of the stuff. Has she always been a rotgut-guzzler?

OLAN. She was a late starter. Didn't touch a drop of the stuff till she was thirty-two, and sure by then she'd had the three of us and fifteen years of biddy-bids behind her. (*Pause*.) The ol' mole was scarred and bruised from top to toe before she resorted to the ol' drink. Ya know she hates the taste of it, don't ya?

AIRNIN. Why is she always suppin' it then, Ol?

OLAN. Helps numb the pain she says, helps her roll with his punches . . .

AIRNIN. Sure, you'd roll with anythin' when you're stocious!

OLAN. Ho, ho, you would indeed!

AIRNIN (*serious*). Ya know she can't stand half the time now, Ol? Most days I'm steerin' her up them stairs in case she falls backwards and breaks her neck.

OLAN. You'd wanna be careful there, Airnin, she's a dead weight when she scuttered. She could take you with her.

AIRNIN. Sure, what choice do I have, boi? I have to help her . . . You're not around half the time . . .

OLAN. Sure, she's gone beyond carin' now anyway. Her ol' dignity's vanishin' by the newtime.

AIRNIN. 'Tis not puttin' a stop to her suppin' though, is it? I keep finding bloody bottles hidden all over the shack. I found a bottle of Powers in the garage.

EANNA. I found a bottle of Paddy in the toilet cistern.

OLAN (*joining in*). I found a bottle of Jameson in the washin' machine . . .

AIRNIN. Nothin' or no one can put a stop to our Mammy's suppin'.

OLAN. Many's a day the Mammy is drunk as a skunk.

EANNA. Many's a day she's badgered.

AIRNIN. Many's a day totally banjaxed.

Pace: increases very gradually throughout the following to an utterly violent hysteria.

OLAN. Battered.

AIRNIN. Befuggered.

EANNA. Bladdered.

OLAN. Blasted.

AIRNIN. Buckled.

OLAN. Burlin.

EANNA. Cabbaged.

AIRNIN. Clobbered.

OLAN. Gatted.

EANNA. Goosed.

AIRNIN. Hammered.

OLAN. Hanging.

EANNA. Jaiked up.

AIRNIN. Lagged up.

OLAN. Langers.

EANNA. Legless.

AIRNIN. Locked out of her mind.

EANNA. Mangled, mashed, mullered.

OLAN. Nicely irrigated with horizontal lubricant . . .

AIRNIN. Off her pickle!

OLAN. Off her trolley!

AIRNIN. On a campaign of it!

OLAN. Out of her tree on it!

ALL. Out of it!
     Out of it!!

OLAN. Paralytic.

EANNA. Pickled.

AIRNIN. Pie-eyed.

OLAN. Plastered.

AIRNIN. Rat-legged.

EANNA. Rat-arsed.

OLAN. Rat-eared.

AIRNIN. Screwed.

OLAN. Scuttered.

EANNA. Slaughtered.

AIRNIN. Smashed.

EANNA. Sozzled.

AIRNIN. Spannered.

OLAN. Steamin'.

ALL. Twisted.
    Tanked.
    Tashered.
    Trashed.
    Wasted.
    Wrecked.
    Wasted!
    Wasted!!
    Wasted!!!
    Wasted!!!!
    Wasted!!!!!

They collapse, totally exhausted.

Pace: slow.

AIRNIN (*curious*). Why do you think the ol' mole stays with
    the Da Da?

OLAN. Pride.

EANNA. Money.

OLAN. Fear.

*Pace: speeding up again, gameshow-like, to *.*

EANNA. Or could it possibly be the swimmin' pool out the back?

OLAN. Or the three new cars out the front?

EANNA. The expensive holidays?

OLAN. Maybe it's her fancy clothes?

EANNA. I'd say it's the fully stocked bar in the sittin' room!! *

AIRNIN (*serious*). She stays because of us.

EANNA. Because of us?

OLAN (*brashly*). She stays because she's proud. Too bloody proud!

EANNA. The Mammy doesn't want to lose face . . .

OLAN. Or the big house, or the money.

EANNA. Not forgettin' the fully stocked bar in the sittin' room!

OLAN. Sure, how could she forget the fully stocked bar in the sittin' room!

AIRNIN (*innocently*). Maybe she wants to save face?

OLAN (*turns on her sharply*). Save face? Oh now, which of the Mammy's faces would that be?

AIRNIN. What are you sayin'?

OLAN (*threateningly*). Jesus, Airnin, can you not just say what ya mean for once? Which of the Mammy's faces is she tryin' to save?

AIRNIN. Olan, sure I don't know what you're sayin'.

OLAN. Is it the big-blue-black-bulging one?

AIRNIN. What?

OLAN (*going for her*). Or the puce-distorted one?

AIRNIN. I don't know what you're talking –

OLAN (*interrupting her, pressing his face to hers*). Maybe it's her blankety-blank-look bleedin' one?

AIRNIN. Please!

OLAN (*losing it*). Or her battered, broken, bloody bruised one?

AIRNIN. Olan, please, stop it!

OLAN (*grabbing her face roughly*). Or whiskey-breath, moon-shaped? Is that the face she's tryin' to save? Is it that one, is it, is it??

AIRNIN *is struggling to break free, her hands over his. She puts up a good fight, but* OLAN *is far stronger.* EANNA *doesn't go to help* AIRNIN – *he is frightened of* OLAN.

EANNA (*from the side*). Olan! Leave her alone! Please. Don't you understand?

OLAN *breaks from* AIRNIN, *who is shaken but trying not to show it.*

OLAN (*incensed*). No, I don't understand!! How the fug can she stay with an animal like that? Jesus Christ Almighty, is she mad or something? (*Shouting.*) What is wrong with her?

EANNA (*very quietly*). She stays because of us, Olan. She says she stays because of us . . .

Long pause.

Pace: slow.

Curled up small, AIRNIN *is 'playing' with* EANNA, *as if he is her baby.*

AIRNIN. Are ya in the Mammy's womb, Eanna?

EANNA (*nodding*). I am.

AIRNIN. Why don't you stay there . . . ?

EANNA. I want to stay here.

AIRNIN. Has the Da Da's already started on ya?

EANNA *nods.*

EANNA *and* AIRNIN (*exactly together*). Thump-o, thump-o – (*Beat.*) thump-o!

Pause.

AIRNIN. You're tiny.

EANNA. I'm only small.

AIRNIN. The smallest . . .

EANNA. And weak. (*Pause.*) He's a big man.

AIRNIN. Biggest in Cork, I'd say.

EANNA (*terrified whisper*). I'm petrified of him.

   Pause.

   Speaking to each other but not hearing each other.

   What are ya doin', cowerin' behind chairs?

AIRNIN. What are ya doin', slidin' under the bed?

OLAN (*joining in*). What are ya doin', curled up in wardrobes?

ALL. Avoiding ya, Da Da. Avoiding ya!

   Pause.

AIRNIN (*gently*). Tip-toe, tippy-tip-tip-toe . . .

EANNA. We're always doin' the tip-toe 'round the Da Da when he's puffed up . . .

OLAN. And the Mammy when she's mangled . . .

AIRNIN. Tippy-tip-toe . . . terrified we'll awaken another brutal onslaught . . .

EANNA (*to* OLAN). Tip-toeing 'round ourselves . . .

AIRNIN. Tip-tip-toe . . .

EANNA (*quietly, to* AIRNIN *and* OLAN). You've both inherited the worst of them.

AIRNIN. Tippy-tip-tip-tip.

EANNA (*to* OLAN). You've his violence about ya, Olan, and – (*Gesturing to* AIRNIN.) and you've the madness of the Mammy.

AIRNIN. Tip-toe, tippy-tip-toe.

OLAN (*to* EANNA). You've their weakness.

AIRNIN. So we tip-toe around them . . .

OLAN (*to* EANNA). The Da Da's been playin' on your weakness for years. Humiliatin' ya in front of us all, and like the fool that ya are you just sit there grateful to him for givin' ya some of his twisted attention . . .

AIRNIN. I pray that the Da Da will die in the night . . .

OLAN (*to* AIRNIN). One day you should run.

AIRNIN. One day I will run . . .

EANNA. Your little heart beatin' tight in your chest.

AIRNIN. . . . . into the arms of someone just like him.

EANNA. Your little arms open wide. Far too trustin'.

OLAN. Children must grow up.

EANNA. Children must grow up, but not before their time.

AIRNIN. I'm tryin' to hold on to my innocence but he's pilferin' it from me.

EANNA. 'Tis a treasure no longer yours . . .

OLAN. Run, Airnin. Run . . .

AIRNIN. One day I might run . . .

Pace: moderate, with bright energy gradually building up to an utter hysteria.

OLAN. Isn't it a wonder nobody notices, all the same?

AIRNIN. Oh, I'd say they notice . . .

OLAN. People are cowards, though . . .

AIRNIN. Selfish to the last . . .

OLAN. Every last one.

AIRNIN (*increasing pace, sardonically*). A decided lack of Catholic compassion –

OLAN. – from the compassionate Christians!

AIRNIN (*as neighbour*). Whatever that family's problems are, I'm sure they'll iron themselves out!

OLAN (*as neighbour*). No need to be interferin' at all – just let the hair sit and all will be fine!

AIRNIN (*as neighbour*). No need to be interferin', at all at all! Sure, haven't we enough problems of our own without bringin' that lot on us? Sure the car wouldn't start this mornin'.

OLAN. 'Twas far from decency those children were reared.

AIRNIN. We'll say a rosary for ya!

OLAN. Sure, we all knew what was goin' on in that house but we didn't want to be interferin'! Sure, these things always iron themselves out.

AIRNIN *and* OLAN (*to* EANNA). Show us your tragic puss!

EANNA *pulls a lunatic victim pose, humorously exaggerating his disability.*

OLAN. Would you look at that tragic puss?

AIRNIN. Sure, what have you to be tragic about?

OLAN. Sure, haven't you a swimmin' pool out the back?

EANNA (*snaps out of it and gets up to join in with them*). And three acres of daisy-free lawn out the front?

OLAN. Sure, you don't know how easy you have it!

AIRNIN. You're too privileged!

EANNA. That's your problem. You're *too* privileged!

AIRNIN (*as herself*). People really don't want to know though, do they? They don't want to be brought down by other people's troubles.

OLAN (*as himself*). They're weak . . .

EANNA (*as himself*). Far too busy confessin' their paltry sins to a lonely man in an ornate box stinkin' of incense.

OLAN. Simply incensed by the insanity of it all! Sure, who ever really sins?

EANNA. Not the ones in confession boxes anyway, cursin' the fact that every week they had to make somethin' up. Jesus Christ, the madness of it all!

OLAN (*as priest*). Ah, we'll take them down a peg or two, sure, isn't that what we're here for?

EANNA (*as priest*). Sure I can't save you, if you won't save yourself.

OLAN. Sure how can I save you if you won't save yourself?

AIRNIN. Crazy logic!

EANNA (*as himself*). Insane reason.

OLAN (*as himself*). The fools, the fools!

AIRNIN. Ah, feck it to hell!

EANNA. Sure, how can I save you, if you won't save yourself?

AIRNIN. Feck it to hell! Feck it to hell!!

OLAN. So no one ever did anything.

AIRNIN. Until it was too late.

EANNA (*as himself*). But then it really was too late!

AIRNIN. So the ol' *faux* guilt sets in.

OLAN. Would ya' look at that guilty puss?

AIRNIN (*pulls manic comic guilty face, then snaps out of it*). Sure, who ever really sins?

OLAN. A nation of hippy-hip hypocrites and deaffy-deaf ears!

EANNA (*to OLAN, mimicked, rhythmic*). Poor you!

OLAN. Poor me!

EANNA (*to AIRNIN*). Poor you!

AIRNIN. Poor me!

OLAN (*to* EANNA). Poor you!

ALL (*with military precision*). God save us all!

'Cos we don't intend to save ourselves,

Lord, save us and guard us!

'Cos it sounds like too much hard work to us,

We've put ourselves in your hands!

'Cos we wouldn't know what hard work is,

Mould us!

Scold us!

Fold us in the clothes of heaven!

Bind us together and beat us, God,

FOR WE HAVE MORTALLY SINNED AGAINST THEE!

Pause.

All three as Teacher, Priest, Neighbour, etc., getting increasingly manic throughout the following.

OLAN. Hey! Whatever else you do you must tell someone if there's a beatin' carryin' on at home.

AIRNIN. You must tell someone, that's what they're always sayin'!

EANNA. Whatever else you do, you must tell someone if that sorta carry-on is carryin' on at home.

OLAN. So I'm tellin' a neighbour.

EANNA. I'm tellin' a teacher.

AIRNIN. I'm tellin' Grandad when he has his hand between my legs fiddlin' with me.

OLAN. What does he say?

AIRNIN. He says, 'Don't tell anybody about this or I'll kill ya!'

EANNA. We don't like that sorta carry-on one little bit!

OLAN. Not one biddy-bid-bit!!

AIRNIN (*losing it*). You must tell! You must tell!!

EANNA (*similarly*). If you don't tell, we can't help ya!!

AIRNIN (*similarly*). How can we help ya if ya don't tell??

OLAN. Sure, if ya tell we'll be here for ya!

EANNA. We'll never let you down!

AIRNIN. We'll take the required action!

EANNA. We'll be strong for you!

OLAN. We'll make him face up to it!

AIRNIN. We'll make him pay for it!

EANNA. We'll take him down!

OLAN. We'll send him packin'!

AIRNIN. Give him a taste of his own medicine. But really –

ALL (*hysterical*). WE'LL DO NOTHIN' AT ALL!!

> *Long pause. They are exhausted.*

> *Pace: starting slow, but building.*

OLAN. I'm gonna kill him.

EANNA. I'm gonna kill him.

OLAN. I'm gonna do it.

EANNA. I am.

OLAN. I am.

EANNA. I am.

OLAN. I AM!!

> *Pause.*

AIRNIN (*a tempo*). You aren't gonna do a thing, Olan.

OLAN (*accusingly*). No?

AIRNIN. No! You're all talk, boi!

OLAN. All talk, eh? (*Sharply, to* EANNA.) Where's his stick?

AIRNIN (*cautioning*). No, Olan, don't!

OLAN. You know, the one with the spikes.

OLAN *is rummaging around to find the stick.*

EANNA. The hawthorn stick?

OLAN (*finding it*). The very one, Eanna boi, the very one!

AIRNIN. I'm tellin' ya, Olan – leave it. He'll kill us if we touch it!

OLAN (*regarding the stick*). D'ya know he's had it specially made for the job? The ol' fugger's only gone and had it deliberately made from the hawthorn, good sharp pointies on it too, ideal for the job in hand, wouldn't ya say, Eanna boi?

He swipes at EANNA*'s legs with the stick.*

Wouldn't ya say??

AIRNIN. If he catches ya with that you're dead.

OLAN (*to* AIRNIN). Would you listen to herself? A whack across the back of the legs with this baby and you'll know who yer talkin' to, girl – you'll be spittin' stars! Nothin' in hell scars as badly as a lash from this – sure look at Eanna here – (*He roughly grabs* EANNA*'s crippled arm.*) Sure, wasn't it the stick that crippled ya, ya poor guffer! Stretch out that arm, ya cripple!

He roughly tugs EANNA*'s arm trying to 'straighten it out'.*

Come on, stretch it out, poncey boy!!

AIRNIN. Olan, leave him alone!

OLAN. The blubberin' Da Da was all remorseful that day up in the hospital! (*As Father.*) Sweet Jesus! I've maimed me own son for life, so I have! (*As himself.*) The fuggin' fugger! I should have laid 'em out right there and had him sent down to the morgue when the job was done!

EANNA. Best place for him, Ol! Best place for him!

OLAN. I'da laid him out alright! I was the man for that job!

AIRNIN (*playfully*). Wishful thinkin', boi, wishful thinkin'!

> OLAN *takes extreme offence at this. He becomes Father and attacks* AIRNIN.

OLAN (*as Father*). Hey, watch your mouth now, girl, no more of your lippy-lip!

AIRNIN. You're all talk, boi!

OLAN. I'm tellin' ya now, watch out, girl, or I'll get my stick to ya and show ya what a beatin' looks like, I'll show ya who's the boss 'round here. (*Puffs himself up.*) I'm the Da Da. I'm the boss 'round here!

EANNA. No, Da Da!

> EANNA *tries to protect* AIRNIN, *who is now looking terrified.*

OLAN. Come here, girl. Come here!!

AIRNIN. No, Da Da! No!!

OLAN. No more of your lippy-lip!

> OLAN, *as Father, chases* AIRNIN, *who puts up a good struggle. He eventually traps her and begins to beat her violently with the stick.*

EANNA (*sardonically, detached, but regarding the others*). The Da Da's always whippin' away at our ankles and arses. Flailin' about like a lunatic! (*Increasingly violent.*) Beltin' us! Beltin' us!!

OLAN. Lick your Da Da's boots! Ya fuggin' girly, ya!

EANNA. That stick is stained with the blood of each of us . . . (*Manic, he can't handle what he's seeing.*) Blood relations. Ha, ha! Hey, hey, never a day, never a day!!

OLAN. Get down on your knees and start lickin'!

> AIRNIN *is on her knees licking her father's boots. He holds the stick poised above her back as a threat.*

EANNA (*mimicking Father*). Get down on your knees this
very instant before I put this stick across your back, and
don't think for a second I wouldn't!!

OLAN. Lick 'em clean, girl, lick 'em clean, I've had enough
of your fuggin' lip!

EANNA (*with jokey Irish gait, fearing him*). Ah, stop, stop!
Sure you wouldn't be up to him, would ya? Oh, he's an
awful case! He's an awful case, I'm tellin' ya now!

OLAN. You've missed a bit!

He jumps back and brings the full force of the stick down on
AIRNIN*'s back. She cracks immediately, her face hits the*
floor and she is splayed out flat.

No more guff out of you now girl. Not so fuggin' smart
now, are ya?

EANNA (*to Father*). You're an animal.

EANNA *runs to* AIRNIN *and tries to cover her body with*
his like a shield. We can see the deep love EANNA *has for*
AIRNIN, *and his guilt over his weakness for not intervening.*
AIRNIN *appears lifeless.*

I'm sorry . . .

Pause.

EANNA *rolls off* AIRNIN, *and curls up with his back to us.*

You're the youngest, Airnin. Aren't ya only small?

AIRNIN (*as a young girl*). I spend my time hidin' from him,
prayin' for a giant wave to come and take us all to a better
place, away from all of this.

EANNA. You sleep lightly, ever ready for war . . .

Pause.

What's that you're seein', Airnin?

AIRNIN. It's the Mammy. She's goin' out the door up the hill.
She's whiskey-stumblin' into the gabbin' neighbour who's
all talk, all questions . . .

EANNA. Just what the poor ol' Mammy needs when she's finally decided to run from the Da Da, eh?

AIRNIN. But the Da Da spots her and reclaims her quick with a sharp –

EANNA. – but discreet –

AIRNIN. – jab in the ribs.

EANNA. The gabbler doesn't suspect a thing.

AIRNIN. The Mammy's indignity reigns; she loses her nerve, loses her mind and slides back down the hill into hell –

EANNA. She stumbles through the door. Scentin' of whiskey, swayin' on her feet. She won't look you in the eye.

AIRNIN. She won't look me in the eye. I'm clingin' to her leg 'cos I think she's come back for me.

EANNA. She won't touch you.

AIRNIN. She won't touch me. She can hardly stand. She's scuttered.

EANNA (*slurred, as Mother*). What was I thinking, love? Sure, how could I forget my angel? Of course I only came back for you . . .

AIRNIN. Take me with you Mammy!

EANNA. But the Mammy laid low. Kept out of his way and crept out after dark, on her own.

AIRNIN. She didn't take me with her . . .

EANNA. . . . . and a curious cold wind whistled through the house.

AIRNIN. I'd learnt my first lesson in loss.

Pause.

Pace: very slow.

OLAN (*whispering*). We.

EANNA. Three.

AIRNIN. Are.

ALL. One.

Pause.

AIRNIN. It could take a lifetime to talk about it . . .

Pace: moderate but increasing to fast. Throughout the following AIRNIN *and* OLAN *become totally unhinged.*

OLAN. You'da think he'da been more careful though, wouldn't ya? Sure, people are sure to spot these sorta things – bruises, broken limbs and the like.

AIRNIN. Do ya think he's tryin' to beat somethin' into us or out of us . . . ?

OLAN. Into us or out of us??

AIRNIN (*winding up, sardonically*). What is it the big man sees in the three of us that he's so keen to rid us of?

EANNA. Himself probably . . .

AIRNIN. You're not the brightest but I'd say you're spot on there, Eanna, spot on, boi!

OLAN (*as Father*). You remind me of all the mistakes I've made, that's why I'm going to pulp ya!

AIRNIN (*similarly*). If only I wasn't such a perfectionist.

OLAN (*similarly*). If only your Mammy didn't drink!

AIRNIN. If only I could relax. I'd be a better man for sure!

EANNA. If only he didn't hate himself . . .

OLAN. That's why I have to pulp ya!

AIRNIN. A better man I'd be for sure and everyone would know about it!

OLAN (*to* EANNA). That's why I'm gonna blast ya!

AIRNIN (*to* EANNA). Belt ya!

OLAN. Bash ya!

AIRNIN. Bruise ya!

OLAN. Batter ya!

AIRNIN. It'll do you no harm!

OLAN. Bruised black-and-blue!

AIRNIN. Blasted!

OLAN. Bashed!

AIRNIN. Battered!

OLAN. I'll teach ya to stand up for yourself!

AIRNIN. A stronger lad you'll be for it!

OLAN. I'll toughen you up!

AIRNIN. I'll toughen you up!

OLAN. You'll thank me for it in the end!

AIRNIN *and* OLAN (*hysterically*). You'll thank me for it!
You'll thank me for it in the end!!

They finally stop and look at each other.

OLAN (*regarding* EANNA). Why did he have to be so weak?

Long pause.

Pace: slow.

OLAN (*directly to* EANNA). Are you my twin?

EANNA (*straight ahead*). She dresses us identically . . .

OLAN. But you can't be. You're older than me.

EANNA. I can't be your twin.

Pause.

OLAN. Why does she dress us the same?

EANNA. She wants you to eclipse me, Olan.

OLAN (*not understanding this*). But I'm not like you.

EANNA. I'm a disappointment to her . . .

OLAN. D'ya know, I'm always feelin' like I have to protect
you, Eanna.

EANNA. You hate my weakness.

OLAN. Yes.

EANNA. You're ashamed of me.

OLAN. I have a duty towards you.

EANNA. A duty you will renege on . . .

OLAN. A duty to look out for you both and protect you from
him.

EANNA (*sardonically*). Because you're the strongest . . .

OLAN. Why are you always hidin' from me?

EANNA. Because you're a bully.

OLAN. Why can I never find you?

AIRNIN (*to* OLAN). You're a bully. (*To* EANNA.) Did the
humiliation of the womb silence ya?

OLAN. What did it do to ya, Eanna?

AIRNIN. What chance did you ever have, kicked in her
blossomin' belly?

EANNA (*detached*). I keep to myself. Just keepin' out of his
way.

AIRNIN. Beaten into this world and out of it . . .

EANNA. I'm not up to the mark.

AIRNIN. . . . into this world . . .

EANNA. So I hide.

AIRNIN. . . . and out of it . . .

EANNA. I'll only ever have one father.

AIRNIN. She says she thought she'd lose you, Eanna. She
could feel you quietin' in her womb, she could feel the fear
grabbin' ya before you even took your first breath.

EANNA. I love him.

AIRNIN. She was bleedin' so heavily that night. Bleedin' the bruised blood so heavily . . .

EANNA. The heart must have been dead inside of him.

AIRNIN (*comforted by his insight*). You don't say much, but you see it all, don't you, Eanna?

EANNA (*matter-of-factly*). His heart was dead.

AIRNIN. She tried to love him but he was an impossible man . . .

EANNA. He was dead.

AIRNIN. A mess of a man.

EANNA. Dead.

   Pause.

AIRNIN. She's started talkin' to the walls in her designer dresses. There's no comin' back from there . . .

Scene Three

Pace: slow.

They are adults.

AIRNIN appears weaker than before, her voice is quieter. OLAN is stooped low with guilt and speaks more gently than before. EANNA is more assured and relaxed than we have previously seen him.

EANNA (*with a smile, not rushed*). Jesus, would you look at the three of us? (*Pause.*) How in God's name did we ever get so far from those snappy days with our little red buckets and spades, the heat of the sun tanning our freckled little arms and the lovely crispy cones of soft ice cream?

OLAN (*to EANNA, gently*). 'Twas a while ago now alright. (*Pause.*) Do you 'member the two of us in our matchin' giraffe tops, Eanna?

EANNA. Jesus, she was always dressin' us the same.

OLAN (*innocently*). Why did she do that?

EANNA (*with a grin*). God knows!

Short pause.

AIRNIN. Such a long time now since she wrapped me in the big warm towel, combin' gently through my hair and singin' to me softly. She useta hold me so carefully, 'twas as if she thought I'd break or somethin'.

Pause. A little faster.

OLAN. Hey, do'ya 'member the Dinky racin' cars, Eanna – you'd the full set, 'member?

AIRNIN (*eagerly*). And there was that board game you were both always playin' –

OLAN. Ah Jesus, yes – what was that called again?

EANNA. 'The Game of Life'.

OLAN. Ha, yes! 'The Game of Life'. (*Pause, a little bitterly.*) The game of life indeed . . .

EANNA. Sure, you were always cheatin' at it!

OLAN. You were easy to fool, Eanna boi.

EANNA (*regarding* AIRNIN). I knew you were cheatin', Olan boi! Somehow the ol' winnin' didn't hold as much for me as it did for you. (*Pause.*) Hey, 'member herself – (*With a nod to* AIRNIN.) swirlin' 'round the livin' room in front of the ol' box?

OLAN (*good-naturedly*). Jesus, how could I bloody forget? Every fuggin' Saturday night when I was trying to watch the match!

EANNA. Jesus, you were always dancin'. Dartin' from one side of the room to the next like the cameras were rollin' or somethin'.

OLAN (*to* AIRNIN). You useta never stop the swirlin', girl!

AIRNIN (*lighthearted and tenderly*). Sure, weren't ye always fightin' over who'd take a spin with me?

OLAN. We were not!

EANNA (*playfully*). Hey, watch yourself now, girl!

OLAN. Watch it!

AIRNIN (*with real affection*). My two big bruised brothers . . . (*Pause.*) I love you both so much you know . . .

EANNA (*blushing*). You do not – you're only saying that now!

OLAN (*to* AIRNIN). Hey, Airnin, you're making him blush – look at him!

EANNA (*hugely blushing*). I am not, go 'way out of that!

OLAN. Hey, ya never lost it, Eanna, ya blusher boy, ya! (*Short pause, then to* AIRNIN.) Jesus, you sure were a live wire.

EANNA (*to* OLAN). D'ya know . . .

OLAN. A really spirited little lass.

EANNA. D'ya know, I . . .

OLAN. Full of the energy, and feisty with it.

EANNA (*intensely, to* OLAN). D'ya know, I miss the smell of her hair?

Pause.

OLAN (*unsure how to respond to this, to* AIRNIN). You were the right ol' tomboy in them days, though, weren't ya?

EANNA. The most glorious long blonde hair . . .

OLAN. A fierce headstrong lassie you were.

EANNA. Ah, she was innocent enough . . .

OLAN. But for all her bloody dancin', wha?

EANNA. She was a treasure. I useta love just watchin' her.

OLAN. You *were* close.

EANNA. Spinnin' and spinnin' . . . I loved –

OLAN (*trying to lighten the tone*). – seein' her cheeky puss?

EANNA (*glorious memory*). Just watchin' her . . .

OLAN (*to* AIRNIN, *playfully*). Hey, Airnin, would ya show us your cheeky puss?

Half-hearted cheeky face from AIRNIN – *she's beyond it now.* OLAN *pulls back; he is shocked by this, and* EANNA *is upset.*

Pause.

EANNA (*intensely, to* OLAN). She's very special to me.

OLAN. Sure, don't I know that?

EANNA. She looked out for me, ya know. Tried hard to protect me as best she could. She was only a little girl.

OLAN (*seriously*). Why did you leave her so?

EANNA (*overlapping, not hearing him*). So why did I leave her?

OLAN. That's a question she's been askin' a long time now. You broke her heart, ya know – snapped the little mite in two. (*Pause.*) Just look at her . . . she's a shadow of herself, Eanna.

Pause, then slow.

EANNA (*ignoring him*). I'm tryin' to remember.

Short pause.

OLAN. I'm tryin' to forget.

Short pause.

AIRNIN (*similarly*). I'm tryin' to make sense of it all.

Slightly longer pause.

(*Innocent realisation.*) Maybe it's time we stopped?

OLAN (*to* AIRNIN). Time we stopped?

EANNA. We still have a way to go, Airnin, we still have a way to go . . .

Short pause.

Pace: faster, a change of mood.

EANNA (*to* OLAN). So Olan, tell me, are you still a wild card?

OLAN (*not unkindly, to* EANNA). Are you still a weaklin'?

AIRNIN (*quickly, pontificating, in a 'posh' Cork voice*). We all did the best that we could in the time that we had and under the circumstances!

OLAN (*seriously*). The Da Da was a nutter, but she must have provoked him. I mean, she wasn't the full shillin', was she?

EANNA. Musta been some provocation for him havin' to resort to tryin' to kill her . . .

AIRNIN. He was a bully.

EANNA. He was brutal.

OLAN. He was selfish . . .

EANNA (*taking issue with* OLAN). He was selfish?

AIRNIN (*to* OLAN). *You* were selfish.

OLAN (*incredulously*). *I* was selfish?

EANNA (*to* AIRNIN). Maybe the Mammy was selfish?

AIRNIN. Selfish and mad.

OLAN. He said *she* was mad.

EANNA. She said *he* was mad.

OLAN (*with ease, to* EANNA). They said you were mad from day one, boi, from day one!

EANNA (*lightheartedly*). What would you know of it?

OLAN (*to* AIRNIN). And you, sweet-face, ya went a bit mad yourself, didn't ya?

AIRNIN (*with humour*). 'Twas the sanest time of my life!

OLAN. Ah now, Airnin – the wit-a wit-a-woo! Ya never lost it, girl, ya never lost it . . .

Pause.

AIRNIN. Come 'ere, would'ya have called the Da Da a workaholic?

EANNA. A perfectionist more like.

AIRNIN. Do you think that's why he was always beatin' us, he tryin' to perfect us?

EANNA (*in a 'posh' voice*). The Da Da showed such admirable ambition, not to mention a viscous determination to perfect us all!

OLAN. Ha, ha!

AIRNIN. Hey, hey!

OLAN. Never a day, day, day!

ALL. Went by, by, by!!

Pause.

OLAN (*suddenly straight*). They should have strangled him at birth.

EANNA (*with concern for him*). Let it go, Olan.

Pause.

Pace: getting slower with each speech.

AIRNIN. I'm tryin' to –

EANNA. – forget, I'm tryin' to –

OLAN. – remember, I'm tryin' to –

AIRNIN. – get away

OLAN. – from it all . . .

Pause.

AIRNIN (*to* OLAN). Is that why you ran?

OLAN (*tensely to* AIRNIN, *challenging*). Is that why you're still running?

Short pause.

AIRNIN (*intensely, to* OLAN). Where *are* you, Olan?

Uncomfortable pause. They hold each other's gaze.

EANNA. Let it go, lads. It's best to let it all go now.

AIRNIN (*again, to* OLAN, *with real intensity*). Where *are* you??

EANNA. We're almost there.

Pause.

Pace: speeds up a little.

OLAN (*as if out of nowhere, seriously*). I've had enough of this.

AIRNIN (*similarly*). I've *heard* enough of this.

OLAN. What am I doing here with you two?

AIRNIN. I'm leavin'. This is pointless.

Long pause. No one moves.

OLAN (*softer, to* EANNA). You planned your exit well.

EANNA (*self-deprecating*). 'Twas the only thing I knew I could do right!

AIRNIN (*sardonically*). You'd had plenty of practice . . .

OLAN (*sharply, to* AIRNIN). He wasn't the only one . . .

AIRNIN (*pained*). We don't talk about that.

OLAN (*challenging*). *You* don't talk about that . . .

EANNA (*in her defence*). But *she's* still here, Olan. (*His voice weakening.*) She's *still* here. (*Pause.*) I was there from the start. (*To* OLAN.) You were there in the middle of it. (*To* AIRNIN.) She were there at the end, tryin' to pick up the pieces – not a pretty sight . . .

OLAN (*softly, with innocent curiosity*). Whatever happened to the ol' Da Da, Airnin?

AIRNIN (*slowly*). The ol' Da Da died by his own hand. (*Pause.*) By his own hand he lit the flame that began to erase it all. (*Pause.*) That began to begin it all. That began to begin to let the blood come out. To let the bruised blood finally come out . . . (*Pause.*) He took everything we had with him.

EANNA (*matter-of-factly*). He always said he would.

AIRNIN. Burnt it all to the ground . . .

OLAN. Some bastard, wha?

AIRNIN. We lost everythin'. Not a stitch on our backs to top it all off.

EANNA. He always said he –

AIRNIN (*interrupting*). One night. (*Short pause.*) One match. Everything was gone . . .

OLAN (*distractedly*). I've been lookin' for him, ya know . . .

AIRNIN. What?

OLAN. Up at nightfall. Down at dawn. Always lookin' for the Da Da.

EANNA (*directly to* OLAN). Sometimes the people you love are very hard to find . . .

Short pause.

OLAN (*directly to* EANNA). I've been runnin' a long time.

EANNA. Ya have.

Short pause.

AIRNIN (*to* OLAN). I've not seen ya in years . . . (*Holds his face.*) Where are ya?

EANNA (*to* AIRNIN). Can't you see he's missin'?

AIRNIN (*her hands tightening on* OLAN's *face*). Olan, where are ya?

OLAN (*ignoring her*). Ya know, sometimes I felt sorry for the Da Da.

AIRNIN. How can you say that?

OLAN. Sometimes, I *did* feel sorry for him.

AIRNIN (*incredulously*). Jesus Christ Almighty, how could you feel sorry for a man like that?

EANNA. Airnin, can't you see –

AIRNIN (*enraged*). Even with his hands tensin' around your tiny neck, his thumbs on your throat, tryin' to squeeze the life outta ya, how in Christ's name could ya say ya felt sorry for him?

OLAN (*to* AIRNIN). How could you not feel sorry for a man like that?

EANNA. – he's still running . . .

AIRNIN (*hysterically, disbelieving*). He tried to kill you!

EANNA (*quietly*). He tried to kill all of us.

AIRNIN. He set fire to you, Olan. He set fire to you, boi!!

OLAN *is visibly humiliated throughout the following.*

Pace: increasing throughout.

OLAN (*pretending not to remember*). That's not true. That never happened.

AIRNIN *exposes* OLAN*'s stomach: terribly scarred flesh.*

AIRNIN. Olan, look at you! How in God's name do you think this happened? Look what he did to you!

OLAN. If I don't remember then it couldn't have happened.

AIRNIN. How can you say you don't remember?

OLAN. We don't speak about it.

EANNA (*quietly*). One day you'll speak about it.

OLAN. I can't remember. This is not my story. (*To* AIRNIN.) Back to you.

AIRNIN (*incredulously*). Back to me?

OLAN (*infuriated*). Isn't that why we're here? A long walk back to yourself from all of this?

He grabs her and violently shakes her.

Isn't that why we're here, Airnin? (*Losing it.*) To help you?

OLAN *is very shaken. He slowly removes his hands from* AIRNIN *and immediately crumbles with guilt.* AIRNIN *is in shock.* EANNA *tentatively stretches out his crippled arm towards* OLAN, *which* OLAN *doesn't see.* EANNA *pulls his hand slowly, back into the crippled position.*

Pause.

Pace: quicker, gradually increasing to *.*

OLAN (*broken*). I can't speak.

EANNA. I say nothin'.

AIRNIN. I say too much, but never the right words . . .

OLAN. I had to leave.

AIRNIN (*to herself*). I couldn't leave.

EANNA (*to himself*). He was tryin' to take me down with him.

AIRNIN. I was only a child.

OLAN (*to himself*). I couldn't stay.

EANNA. I couldn't go.

OLAN. He was tryin' to break me.

AIRNIN. Where could I have gone?

EANNA. I couldn't breathe.

OLAN. I wouldn't let him break me.

EANNA. It was killin' me.

AIRNIN (*becoming upset*). I was only a child.

EANNA. Killin' me . . .

OLAN. Don't make me remember what I need to forget.

AIRNIN (*with great upset*). Don't make me remember! *

    Pause.

OLAN (*to* EANNA, *with concern for* AIRNIN). Maybe it's time we stopped?

EANNA (*warning*). She must go on.

OLAN. Who are you to say that?

EANNA. She must go on. Isn't that why we're here?

OLAN. Where have *you* been?

    Pause.

AIRNIN. The Mammy always said Eanna was a dark child. I never knew just how dark. (*Pause.*) A winter child . . . She knew he'd never survive spring.

OLAN (*to* AIRNIN, *regarding* EANNA). He didn't last long, did he?

AIRNIN (*pained*). I can't talk about him.

OLAN (*to* EANNA). Do you know, we never talk about you? (*To* AIRNIN.) Why don't we ever talk about him, Airnin?

AIRNIN (*becoming tense*). I can't think about him.

EANNA. Maybe you should . . .

OLAN (*to* AIRNIN). Why don't we?

AIRNIN. Don't!

EANNA. I can still hear you both, ya know.

OLAN. Talk to him, he can still hear you.

AIRNIN. Don't make me, please, Olan!

EANNA. I could see no other way out of it all. I was tormented.
I'm sorry, I . . .

AIRNIN (*interrupting*). Jesus, no!

EANNA (*gently*). Don't be scared, Airnin. Sure, I've been
dead a long time now . . .

OLAN. We'll have to speak about him . . .

AIRNIN. No!

OLAN (*to* AIRNIN, *angrily, accusing*). Why not?

AIRNIN. I *can't* remember him.

OLAN. What are you sayin', Airnin?

EANNA (*innocently, as if everyday*). D'ya know, death's a
really lonely place . . . I didn't think it would be, so many
people went before us, ya know? So many people I thought
I'd meet again . . . D'ya know I can't find any of them here
and I've been lookin' for a long time . . .

OLAN. Does your life really pass before your eyes just before
you die?

EANNA. Yes.

OLAN. The good bits or the bad?

EANNA (*emotionally*). The bad mostly, but it doesn't last
long.

Pause.

OLAN. Do you regret how you left us, Eanna?

EANNA *nods*.

(*Pressing, anxiously.*) Do you regret any of it?

EANNA. I regret leavin' ya both.

AIRNIN (*reliving it*). It was weeks before they found you. The smell . . . I touched you.

Totally overcome by this, she is beginning to break down.

Your body was so cold. For the first time in my life I was scared of you. I hardly recognised you, boi. Jesus, I can still smell that room – after so long on your own.

OLAN (*emotionally, squeezing* EANNA). I miss ya, boi.

EANNA. I haven't spoken to anyone since the night I died, I've been waitin' for this night for a long time, ya know?

Long pause. The three of them cling to each other in grief.

AIRNIN (*singing, childlike, to the tune of 'The Connemara Cradle Song'*).
'Down in the valley, walking between,
Telling our story, here's what it means.
Here's what it means, love, here's what it means,
Telling our story, here's what it means . . . '

Pause.

OLAN (*to* EANNA). I left her too. I thought the runnin' would save me, so that's what I did. Like so many men before me. I ran. Far. Wild. Free. I'm still runnin'. (*Nods to* AIRNIN.) She thinks I'm missing, which I am, but not in the way she thinks. (*Longer pause.*) I was there the night she died . . . (*Pause.*) and the mornin' she was revived. The doctors said they'd never seen anythin' like her dark stubbornness to stay in this pitiless world. (*Pause.*) She's been in and out of hospitals and homes – she has no trust or faith in anyone, and fragile enough underneath it all. I've heard she's scarred, much more than just what's visible, she's less than a shadow of the spirit she used to be. Sure, how could she be anythin' else after what she's seen and the loss she's had? (*Pause.*) I haven't seen her in twenty years now. But I hear

she's like a beautiful bird in a cage. Dyin' for freedom. Ever
a slave. (*Breaking down, overcome with guilt.*) She sings, oh
yes she sings, but her songs are dark indeed . . . Songs of
loss and unspeakable things. Songs of loss and unspeakable
things . . . (*Pause.*) I am missing, but not in the way she
thinks. Just a man, broken by guilt, broken by his own
hands. A missing man . . .

*Pace: moderate, never rushed. The spoken text should
overlap with the song.*

OLAN *sings.*

'Bird in a cage, love, bird in a cage,
Dying for freedom, ever a slave.
Ever a slave, love, ever a slave,
Dying for freedom, ever a slave . . . '

OLAN *and* EANNA *hum the melody very quietly, loosely,
as* AIRNIN *speaks.*

AIRNIN. I dreamt of you both again last night. I'm startin' to
think my dreams are reality. I'm losin' sight of you both.
Can you hear me at all? (*Pause.*) I started this in sunlight,
now the night is fallin' and the darkness is settlin' in around
me still, drivin' these memories ever nearer the surface.
(*Becoming tormented.*) This song in my head is makin' my
memories spin, spin, spin. Am I ever a slave to this? Am I
ever a slave to this?

The silence that greets these questions overwhelms AIRNIN
with fear.

I'm losin' you, boys . . . I'm forgettin' your faces . . . 'Tis
like you never existed! Jesus help me, don't let my memories
of them fade. (*Pause.*) Don't let them fade! Allow me just
one sweet image of their little faces without pain . . .

Pause.

EANNA (*smiling, warmly, in a kind whisper*). Sure, look at us
so . . .

OLAN (*similarly*). Aren't we here now for you?

AIRNIN. You're fadin' from me. Stay with me, please?

OLAN. You'll have to go onwards alone.

AIRNIN. I can't go any further!

EANNA. The memories will fade if you let them . . .

OLAN. See the cross . . .

AIRNIN. Stay with me!

OLAN. See the cross, Airnin, that's your burden . . .

AIRNIN. Watch over me, tonight of all nights, 'cos I feel I'm . . .

OLAN. That's what causing you all the pain . . .

EANNA. You must go on . . .

AIRNIN (*petrified*). Is this the end?

OLAN. We three are one. Remember that, Airnin.

EANNA. See the cross . . . Shoulder it . . .

OLAN. A long walk back to yourself, wasn't that it?

AIRNIN. With you both at my side . . .

EANNA. A long walk back to yourself –

AIRNIN. 'Hello warriors', that's how it should be.

OLAN. – through the solitary shapes and the shadows –

AIRNIN. Hello warriors . . .

OLAN. – that's how it *will* be, eventually.

EANNA. We look forward to your company again . . .

AIRNIN (*beginning to break*). But I don't want to be here alone.

EANNA. What do you want, Airnin?

AIRNIN. I can't leave . . .

EANNA. Airnin?

AIRNIN. I can't stay!

OLAN (*overlaps*). Can you see it?

EANNA. Can you see it, Airnin? (*To* OLAN.) She must go on.

AIRNIN. I'm lost!!

They hold her. She is terrified.

(*Breaking.*) Is it just us left?

Silence. They are gone.

Is it just us left? Boys? Where are you??

The End.

David Edgar
ALBERT SPEER
CONTINENTAL DIVIDE
EDGAR: SHORTS
PENTECOST
PLAYING WITH FIRE
THE PRISONER'S DILEMMA
THE SHAPE OF THE TABLE

Stella Feehily
DUCK
O GO MY MAN

Chris Fittock
RED

Debbie Tucker Green
BORN BAD
DIRTY BUTTERFLY
STONING MARY
TRADE & GENERATIONS

Tony Kushner
ANGELS IN AMERICA – PARTS ONE & TWO
CAROLINE, OR CHANGE
HOMEBODY/KABUL

Owen McCafferty
CLOSING TIME
COLD COMFORT
DAYS OF WINE AND ROSES *after* JP Miller
MOJO MICKYBO
SCENES FROM THE BIG PICTURE
SHOOT THE CROW

Lisa McGee
GIRLS AND DOLLS

Arthur Miller
AN ENEMY OF THE PEOPLE *after* Ibsen
PLAYING FOR TIME

A Nick Hern Book

Tilt first published in Great Britain as a paperback original in 2007
by Nick Hern Books Limited, 14 Larden Road, London W3 7ST
in association with The New Works

Tilt copyright © 2007 Ailis Ní Ríain

Ailis Ní Ríain has asserted her right to be identified as the author
of this work

Typeset by Country Setting, Kingsdown, Kent CT14 8ES
Printed and bound in Great Britain by Biddles, King's Lynn

A CIP catalogue record for this book is available from
the British Library

ISBN 978 1 85459 981 0

Amateur Performing Rights Applications for performance,
including readings and excerpts, by amateurs in English throughout
the world should be addressed to the Performing Rights Manager,
Nick Hern Books, 14 Larden Road, London W3 7ST,
fax +44 (0) 20 8735 0250, *e-mail* info@nickhernbooks.demon.co.uk,
except as follows:

Australia: Dominie Drama, 8 Cross Street, Brookvale 2100,
fax (2) 9905 5209, *e-mail* dominie@dominie.com.au
New Zealand: Play Bureau, PO Box 420, New Plymouth,
fax (6) 753 2150, *e-mail* play.bureau.nz@xtra.co.nz
South Africa: DALRO (Pty) Ltd, PO Box 31627, 2017 Braamfontein,
tel (11) 489 5065, *fax* (11) 403 9094, *e-mail* Wim.Vorster@dalro.co.za

Professional Performing Rights Applications for performance by
professionals in any medium and in any language throughout the
world should be addressed in the first instance to Nick Hern Books,
14 Larden Road, London W3 7ST, *fax* +44 (0) 20 8735 0250,
e-mail info@nickhernbooks.demon.co.uk.

No performance of any kind may be given unless a licence has been
obtained. Applications should be made before rehearsals begin.
Publication of this play does not necessarily indicate its availability
for performance.